–Calamity Joe–

–Calamity Joe–

Poems by

Brendan Constantine

Red Hen Press | Pasadena, California

Calamity Joe

Book design and layout by Andrew Mendez

Library of Congress Cataloging-in-Publication Data

Constantine, Brendan.

Calamity Joe : poems / by Brendan Constantine.—1st ed.

   p. cm.

 ISBN 978-1-59709-176-3

 I. Title.

 PS3603.O5579C35 2012

 811'.6—dc23

                    2011041860

The Los Angeles County Arts Commission, the National Endowment for the Arts,
and Los Angeles Department of Cultural Affairs partially support Red Hen Press.

Published by Red Hen Press

www.redhen.org

First Edition

Acknowledgements

The author gratefully acknowledges the publishers of periodicals, anthologies, and chapbooks in which some of these poems first appeared:

2River View, "The Boy Has Come Back" & "I Dreamt I Was Your Finger"; *Antenna*, "Joe Dreams Of The Old Man & The Sea" (published as "A Dream About Going"); *The Bicycle Review*, "The Legend of Joe (Just then a team of child Archeologists . . .)"; *The Boxcar Poetry Review*, "Flight Out Of Guest Bedroom"; *Bright Wings: An Anthology of Poems About Birds*, "Rara Avis"; *The Cortland Review*, "Litany"; *Crimewave*, "The Body", "Dies Irae"; *Dante's Casino*, "New Math"; *Ducts.org*, "A Horse Named Death"; *Ploughshares*, "Difficult Listening Time"; *Redivider*, "Before The Flood"; *Verse Wisconsin*, "The Legend of Joe (What the hell else was he gonna do . . .)", *Zombie Dovecote*, "In The Shrine Of The Mynah Bird".

For Mary Katherine Byrne
1955 – 2011

Table of Contents

ONCE

The Cast (in order of disappearance)   13
Prelude   19
Difficult Listening Time   20
The Legend Of Joe   21
The Intervention   22
Before The Flood   24
SPLAY   26
The Horse You Rode In On   28
The Drowned Brother   29
The Legend Of Joe   31
JOE   32
The Calamities   There they are   33
                   An Animal Hospital   34
                   The sick, the injured, the slow   35
                   There they are again   36
                   Give you back   37
                   Nobody's daddy but my own 38
                   Lily   39
                   We left the room and didn't   40
                   This is Calamity   41
                   The words   42

TWICE

The Search Party   45
Litany   46
The Legend Of Joe   48
A Horse Named Death   49
In the Shrine Of The Mynah Bird   50
Rara Avis   51
Joe Dreams Of The Old Man & The Sea   53
The Missing Girl's Horse   55
Supplement–The Old Man Lets Us Have It   57
Compline   61
The Legend Of Joe   62
JOE AGAIN   63
The Formalities My mother ate Queen Anne   64
                   My brother once held up   65
                   My father used to swim   66
                   You   67
                   Go gentle,   68
                   Out there the words are black   69
                   Grief   70
                   Bring the old man downstairs,   71
                   I don't remember why   72
                   Consider the spiders   73
                   The Japanese beetle   74
                   Understand this,   75

THE CHARM

SHIP YOUR HORSE		79
New Math		81
The Legend Of Joe		83
My Favorite Story Is This One		84
The Body		85
A Brief History of The Theater		87
Tragoedia		88
Flight Out of Guest Bedroom		89
RETREATISE		91
The Legend Of Joe		92
JOE ONE MORE TIME		94
The Calm	A dead man doesn't walk into a bar	96
	The shape of my name	97
	Swear	98
	The boy in the next room is mine	99
	Which brings us to God	100
	How many doors	101
	I've found an answer in the bones,	102
	I dreamt I was your finger,	103
	Know this:	104
	Poem	105
	The boy has come back,	106
	Cover your eyes,	107
Dies Irae *(Day of Wrath)*		108

The Cast *(in order of disappearance)*

Z.   The Cancer

First as a spot on the mother's neck but soon spread to the kitchen. It's survived by the living room.

Y.   The Mother

A good story when the old man feels like telling it: "She could peel fruit in her pocket."

X.   The Brother

More beautiful than sleep. Just now, he's sleeping us off.

W.   The Old Man

Wanted to be Dr. Williams but wasn't. Can wheel himself to the liquor store in one song. The doctor, the bank, & the bookie need two songs each.

V.   The Boy

A word, then a shape, then somehow a ship at full sail, trawling the sun. Ahoy!

U.   The Nine-fingered Girl

Delivers world history almost entirely from memory. The rest she makes up. She could use a dress with pockets.

T.   The Lily

Like all gardens; the less said the better.

S–D. *The Cops, Doctors, Nurses,* *Disappear first as a wind, but the landlord*
 Firemen, Watchmen, Waitresses, *is not in the wind: & then an earthquake,*
 Postmen, Masons, Bird Watchers, *but the landlord is not in the earthquake:*
 The Mayor, Townsfolk, Drifters, *& then a fire & the landlord comes, a still*
 Hop Heads, Thieves, Thomas *small voice. They all burn away.*
 Edison & The Landlord

C. *The Animals* *Roles originated by drifters who came to*
 resent it. Later replaced by the real things,
 humid of eye & unbelievably yielding.

B. *The Light* *Dedicates her performance to the vigorous*
 rubbing of two darknesses together.

A. *Calamity Joe* *There he goes.*

14

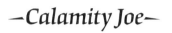

—*Calamity Joe*—

—Once—

"What is done out of love lies beyond good and evil."
—Friedrich Nietzsche

"Friedrich Nietzsche was stupid and abnormal."
—Leo Tolstoy

Prelude

There used to be a house
    where you're standing

you wear the ghost
    of a favorite piano

Though all you know is broken
    earth, trumpet vine,
        Lily Of The Valley,

there is a black dog beside you
    who wants to know
        how you got in

Difficult Listening Time

A flock of pink flamingos moved in
across the street, and set up plastic people
on the lawn.
                        They've faced them out
this way, hands molded to their chins,
looking more like us as night comes on.

Downtown, the waitresses are starving
in their aprons; the watchmen get fainter
by the hour.
                        It's Difficult Listening Time,
object response time, time for 'the tears
of things.'
        There has to be a way to help
it along, a way to dry the rain as it falls
so we can keep these clothes.
                                        Let's go
to the woods & hang a painting of this
room on every tree. We'll go to sea
& on each sailboat fix a picture
of a hotel bed.
                        Or how about we stay
home & talk out every song between us
until we sound like heavy, stupid birds.

The Legend Of Joe

Once there was a man who worked in a lab
because he couldn't afford to keep pets
What the hell else was he gonna' do

The virus loves us, the virus loves us not;
you might as well get paid to find out
Once there was a man who worked in a lab

but that was before the city was burned
to make room for orange groves
What the hell else were we gonna' do

Once there was a mouse who tested average,
a mouse who preferred crosswords to mazes
Once there was a man who worked in a lab

because he didn't work anywhere else
Every day the world turned away from him
What the hell else was it gonna' do

The earth takes everyone personally
whether you hold your breath or sell it
Once there was a lab where no one worked
and the mice piled up like fruit

The Intervention

My mother is out for bear
    Even bought a house
in the woods She says
    the books came after,
says she's just learning
    to avoid bears, but I know
too much She wants one

Wants to lure it into her
    red truck and drive
to a hotel in town
    where she won't have
to whisper the questions
    she's been living to ask

What is your worst memory
of childhood? Why didn't
my father come home
from the war? What stopped
you from killing me when
I was a snow-blind girl?

This is what I wish I didn't
 know: she won't expect
the bear to answer It's not
 the point What'll matter
is her hand on its shoulder,
 the sparkle of silt in its coat,
the shape of its dank eyes
 trying to look away

Before The Flood

My father remembers nothing. Or rather
he remembers where it used to be—*See*
that building? When I was a kid there was
nothing there. And next door, where
the school is,   nothing.

We walk through his hometown, down
a street with an Indian name no Indian
lives to translate. *It means Dream River,*
he says, *or Rambling, Confused River,*
I used to know.
                        No one believes
their parents were children. That is, you
need more than their word. They have to
do something: stifle laughter, cry into
their hands, stand tiptoe. We all look

younger on tiptoe. My father peers
over a fence, another new building.
This was all sand, he says, *for Bethlehem,
Bethlehem Steel*. His shoe is untied.
He bends to lace it, I almost help. Later

I reach for his hand at a crosswalk.
Let's go back, he says. To how
it was? *No, to the house; I need
to lie down*. We turn and the town
surges under our feet, comes over us

in a wooden tide. I get my arms under his,
kick for both of us. He doesn't try,
doesn't speak when his house goes by.

SPLAY

Policemen trace our bodies in chalk

    —so they can put you back if no one claims you
    —because history is knowing where people fell
    —because they're children

Since the first night, the moon's been backing off;
like a possum, a boat, the single headlight
of a hit-and-run driver.

Call an ambulance; there's been a terrible purpose.

Hummingbirds die in the air. Look at the drunken wasp
waving her bottle, the treachery of morning glories;
Eden must have been a slum.

Drink from a cracked cup, the other cups will trust you.

The Big Bang is easier to understand if you know
it was rehearsed. Like this: stand on a pair of crutches
in front of a large mirror. Now, tell yourself not to stare.

You gonna' cry?
You gonna' tell the sky your town is falling?

The ground can't wait to meet us. The wind wants us
in its way. Somewhere a child is tracing a doll.
Chalk has nothing to say.

Every day the sun gets closer; a golden retriever,
a scratched coin, the paper mask of a doctor.

The saddest facts are evidence of joy.

What does the blood say? *Stay inside.* What does
the breath say? *Come back soon.* What does the skull say
under the face? *Smile, smile, smile.*

The Horse You Rode In On

found this town without any help from you,
unless you own how he learned to walk
contrary to your lead, because you never
know where the Hell you're going.

You whipped all the color from his flanks,
only a few grey clouds remain, a storm
under your saddle & star-shaped spurs.

All day he sleeps in his cheap rented stable,
not drinking, not eating his cheap rented oats,
dreaming of the day you hurt him home.

The Drowned Brother

They fished you out yesterday. A hook
in the dragnet passed through your lip,
brought you up to me like a mackerel.

What are cops thinking when they look
down like that? Do they see themselves
in the mirrors of their shoes, make eye
contact there, or are they waiting for
some stammering angel to pass.

        They brought me
your shirt & pants folded in a box.
Were you wearing shoes & socks,
& who dried your clothes?
           I see them,
wet on a line with other shirts & pants,
thousands, hung by old police women
in blue aprons, pulling blue pins
from their cinched mouths.

They got your pleats all wrong.

The lawyer still has your note. *To study*,
he says. How many times must he read it
to have it down? I got, *Gone Fishing*,
on my first try.

Will he send it back
with edits? Can I make you clearer,
develop you more? What of your hair,
your eyes?
                    Were you like anything else?

The Legend Of Joe

Once there was a man who worked in a lab
because he couldn't sing He sang all day
at his microscope—*Hang out the stars*
in Indiana, to light my way back home
to you—to the cancers & sclerosi, to cells
making cells eating cells He sang so loud,
so high, so fatally out of tune, the immuno-
deficient mice put their paws on their ears
& winced

You haven't lived, he would say to them,
until you've done what you love wrong
What they loved was eating road maps,
something they never knew

If I could sing, the man wondered, would I
do science on the side Would I keep a little
microscope backstage—*So look for me in*
Indiana, when the long, long day is through—
Way down the eyepiece a virus was dancing
in a spotlight

JOE

JOE:
Joe?

JOE:
Yes, Joe.

JOE:
Cops are here, Joe.

JOE:
Cops are always here.
You're just looking out the window.

JOE:
Yeah, well anyway Joe…

JOE:
Yeah, Joe?

JOE:
You still thinking about a dog?
You gonna feed the old man?
You gonna put that flower in a vase?

JOE:
Close the window.

The Calamities—

There they are

Police in the yard, hunting for God

knows what. Police in the air, tied

to a man by a strand of light. Police

at school. Police in the pool. Run,

don't run with a gun in your mouth

or your eyes will stay that way.

O see under the tree—police car,

hungry as an animal hospital.

An Animal Hospital

Hunts by waiting, and everywhere—

a desert, a forest, a city. Will bring

its own garden but never hides.

Hunts by waiting and nowhere sleeps,

creeps, or keeps a mate. Bears

no young. Has no call, no call.

Hunts by waiting and everywhere—

the sick, the injured, the slow.

The sick, the injured, the slow

Make a living anyway they can't;

not hunting, not arresting, not keeping

anything down. Tell you the chicken

wanted to be soup more than flying.

Ask you to carry them to the family

room, so they can have a little day.

O Grandfather clock, tap out your pipe;

there they are.

There they are again

Pulling my brother from his car,

through the window of his bottle

glutted car. One officer holds his head

like he means to run off with it.

Another, a woman, has him round

the waist, shouts at him to unhook

his ankle from the wheel. *Stop*

fighting and we'll give you back.

Give you back

Give you back, give you back

my baby. Your chicken's got one

eye, your dog's as deaf as hope,

your cows are floating sideways

on the sweet meadow tide.

Your boy's in my apartment

but he doesn't want to stay.

I'm nobody's daddy but my own.

Nobody's daddy but my own

Looking for love? SWM 15 yrs 5'7"

Slender build. Honest, sensitive,

allergic to nuts, seeks spotted pony.

Want to watch TV? Me—96 5'10"

interested in soup, lawn chairs, love.

You—ageless, faceless, unnamed,

able to carry me from room to room.

Wanted: single lily for handsome vase.

Lily

Doesn't look too good—half closed,

nodding. Open a window or a book,

get a cross-draft going, some answers.

Days ago when she was little

friends would drop by to talk

or sing or weep and she'd keep

open or try to and fall asleep.

We left the room and didn't.

We left the room and didn't

See the animals again. Someone else

took their bodies away. But once

I found a pink leather collar—it must

have come off in the shuffle or struggle,

they do that sometimes, if the smoke

is too weak. I took it home to harm

my heart with its heart-shaped charm:

This is Calamity, please bring her home.

This is Calamity

My brother dragged away like a fortune,

my father confined for decay, all

crawlers of the ark drowned in their plot—

less dreams to make room. *Calamitas*—

between *Caetera*: the rest of anything

and *Calamus*: anything hollow—an arrow,

pipe, or pen. Calamity: to be lost between

what happens and the word for it.

The words

Don't want to be found. They want to

watch. I carry a whole man to a bed

and the words don't help. The police

play a song my brother tries to sing,

but the words go quietly. Tonight

I bury a dog with a lily. The words sit

on bicycles beyond the streetlight. I will

bring them here by their filthy wrists.

–Twice–

"The owl beats the drum on the arch of Afrisiab,
The spider acts the usher in the palace of Caesar."
—Sheik Saadi-I-Shirazi

The Search Party

I got invited to a search party. I dressed all wrong,

brought a gift. It was like a party turned inside

out; we met in a field, walked instead of mingled,

there was no cake. We each got a long candle

we couldn't blow out & had to share one wish

between the hundred of us for the guest of honor

to jump out from a hay loft or behind a big tree

& yell, Surprise. It went on way too long, looking

in ditches, dragging the river, calling. By first light

the honoree still hadn't shown. Half the guests

vowed to stay, the rest took their candles home.

I still have my gift. It's a book.

Litany

Why do we say Good Morning like a command
when we know it won't sit still? Why Good Night
when it won't be flattered?

Why do we whisper in the presence of trees or remove
our shoes to step on the skirt of the sea?

And why do we think of the lake as lonely
when the call of the duck does not echo?
Not even in the chambers of the heart.

Why do we treat infinity as old, as something
we may look into, when we know it is a teenaged boy
who looks no one in the eye?

See what fire does to the hands, water
to the brain, blood to the color of anything;
why do we pretend God isn't an animal,
a big black beetle, antlered for the hoisting of stars?

Infinity keeps her in a box of sand, feeds her silence.
She in turn creates worlds that do not endure
so he'll feel older, grown up.

While we're at it, the sun and the moon have never
risen to greet anyone. The forest does not hear
gossip. The ocean prefers to dance alone.

And none are more abandoned than we who wait
in a wilderness for the children we have been
to lead us out.

The Legend Of Joe

Once there was a man who worked in a lab
cleaning cages because he didn't know why
The lab tested beauty products on animals
hair spray lip stick eye shadow perfume oils
Every day the animals got made up to go out
& died waiting for the car
              The man decided
he would secretly repair the animals when
the scientists finished making them beautiful
At night he washed their coats & eyes, healed
their skin, hummed softly as he stroked them
After a while the lab noticed the animals
weren't dying & deemed all the products
to be safe
              Pretty soon the police came
& took some of the scientists away yelling
Everyone else got fired The man tried
to free the animals but he was stopped
Where are you going with this dog & this
monkey & this rabbit & all these mice
& bugs he was asked

              It's Lady's Night, he said

A Horse Named Death

The man said what else could he name him, the beast
had no color. *Lethal White* it's called because the things
hardly live a whole day. But this one got up.
He raised himself like a church and made for the dark
of the barn, not a whiff to his mother. We didn't think
she'd take to him, but she followed him back there
and began to teach.

                     You can tell a racehorse by his gait;
this one could drag a tractor out to sea. Not that it mattered.
Not like you could get a jock to go near him. A horse
that could only race at night? A horse with red eyes?
A homebred named for the end of times, not to mention
the sport? It was worse than blasphemy. What could he do,
the man asked us. What did God expect him to do?

So the man races him against us. You're driving home
by one of his fields, you can't avoid his fields, just trying
to push aside enough night to get to bed, and the horse
comes. He flashes up beside you like a bedside lamp,
like a secret you thought was kept. Even if you don't stop
to breathe into your hands he passes you. If you speed up
and curse him for every lie you ever told, he passes you.
He passes you like you're falling the other way.

In the Shrine of the Mynah Bird

We, the devout, go one at a time
for there's only one pew.
It's small.

I came because the sign said
    Welcome   Welcome
& stayed to marvel
at the altar—a sewing table,
an empty cage, no candles,
the door the only light.

I let my shadow grow awhile
in the sawdust, then rose
and said aloud,

I don't believe in you.

Beyond the thin bars a trapeze
lightly swang & a voice
small as a telephone's
answered

Who's a clever boy?
        Who's a clever boy?

Rara Avis

When interviewed, the bird watchers were tight–
lipped. One actually got up and left.
When interviewed, the bird watchers gave
quick, birdlike answers. We had to ask many
of our questions twice.
When interviewed, the bird watchers wore hoods.
When interviewed, the bird watchers had this
to say, *We are no more boring than scientists*
or stonemasons. Indeed, many of us are scientists
and stonemasons. Or we could be.
When interviewed, the bird watchers ate crow.
When interviewed, the bird watchers refused
to discuss themselves, preferring to debate
recent observations of the Dope Warbler,
the Spoon Tailed Ninny, the Royal Bavarian
Snack Rail, whether any would survive
another New Hampshire winter.
When interviewed, the bird watchers sucked eggs.
When interviewed, the bird watchers placed
blame squarely on the coal industry.
When interviewed, the bird watchers turned
on each other. It was ugly, like a stoning.
When interviewed, the bird watchers began
to undress, slowly, as if half asleep.
When interviewed, the bird watchers freaked:

one threw handfuls of dirt at the cameras,
another wept uncontrollably.
When interviewed, the bird watchers were small.
When interviewed, the bird watchers blushed
like startled lovers, like priests and nuns.
When interviewed, the bird watchers varied
in their appraisal of the year's display. One
called it *bounteous, rich.* But another seemed
confused, described the birds as *cumulous,*
the weather as *sinusoidal.*
When interviewed, the bird watchers appeared
to be holding back, hiding something.
When interviewed, the bird watchers agreed
to be interviewed again.
The birds could not be reached for comment.

Joe Dreams Of The Old Man & The Sea

I was in a car with my father
& we were going
He was singing *La donna é mobile*
I was in the passenger seat
trying to take in all of him

I couldn't do it
so I looked out the window
We were in the middle of an ocean
Great foaming waves opened
against the car
while small fish tried to avoid us

I got scared
Not because we were at sea
in a Buick
I was scared because
my father was driving way too fast

I started to warn him
but when I looked at him
he had changed into someone else,
a friend of mine from school
He was a boy named Dave
killed on prom night

The ocean turned pink,
then red as fruit punch
I told him to slow down
Why, he asked
Because you're dead
He said, *Yeah*
but I'm OK to drive

So we kept going
We didn't see a cop for days

The Missing Girl's Horse

We went through her bed, over and over,
but she wasn't in it. I turned the sheets
myself, while her mother waved a hand
above the pillow. There was nothing.
We went through her clothes, reaching
into every dress and stocking. We found
none of her. Then her brother went outside
to search the barn. Her horse was awake,
but shook his large head when asked
if he'd seen her. We sent for the Sheriff,
showed him the empty clothes and bed.
He even looked beneath it. *No girl*, he said.
Her mother began to sob into her sleeve;
if only her husband were alive, he would,
he would, he would, he would find her.
I made my face look strong and went back
out to the barn. The horse was mumbling
there. I told it to come clean, shook my fist
and said I already knew. It was a lie, but
it worked, the horse broke down and cried.
I don't know why, he said, *I threw her,*
threw her off in the dusty blue sage. Let her
sleep where she landed, then ran to
put myself into my stall, to find a spot
to stare at in the wall, but I couldn't make it

all into a dream. We ran into the field.
Her mamma called her name, the Sheriff
called for help. Soon we were two dozen
heads and shouts, but the missing girl stayed
missing. The horse showed himself out.

Supplement—The Old Man Lets Us Have It

My people,
       my beloveds,
              my fat and lovely hands
I will teach you to die vicariously
through other men,

through forests of men, to walk
through the costumed lightning we call
humanity. Let us begin

with a road, most contagious
of inventions (after the hammer),
my fat people,
       my lovelies,
              my beloved hands,
a road made from the earth of Texas, 1934.

Here was the first lecture on the subject
given by my father, handkerchiefing
chocolate from my nose, his voice
a boy's, ten boys, (a fat and lovely hand
       itself), pinched my ear
"The rangers have brought justice
to Bonnie & Clyde. They have brought them
as they've killed them to Dallas, to teach us

the value of a dollar. Look well, my son.
Mind your father; don't father your mind."

I see it still, blink out dust and sugar,
swallow a surge of blue, blink on again
the rangers smoking crude cigarettes,
smoking crudely around the tow truck,
the Death Car behind it, the maybe oil
probably blood leaking from it to answer
the sky in patches
                    so nasty,
                    dark.

So much wheels
upon

the dead Clyde
Barrow

poised on red
leather

beside the white
woman.

Because the dead are each a finger
on a many armed, chimeless clock,
to regard them is to read the hour,
            to call the hour,
                    to chime to one's self.

                    Let us resume. The sunniest
day is nothing compared to the movies,
the fat and lovely movies
of summer. Have you seen the one
about the man, the woman, the mis-
understanding?
            It is a remake
of a classic, based on a book,
inspired by a song which began as a poem
cried in the mouth of a neighbor,
cried *Help, police* . . .

There was a sequel
half as good as the first.

My hands,
        my people,
                    my fat, lovely love
see it now,
someday you may play a role in the re-remake.

But let us say you have no money,
cannot afford films or field trips,
have no father, eat photographs
to survive, must you only live?

I tell you, No.
Make a window with your famous hands,
look through it to the street.
There should be men.
If not, certainly news-
papers.

At the top of page one, above the war,
the bugle, even the year and day
add this word–POEMS

                    It is easy
to get poetry from the news
                Yet men write miserably every day
                        upon learning it.
The trick is triage;
put your name at the bottom of each death,
            they are yours for the reading.
                    Read them now.

Compline

Perhaps it was the eyelashes we added to the scarecrow,   a fence post
that never healed,   or that what we thought was a sweetness of wind
& grass was really   hissing.   No matter, the house is burning now.
We're powerless to save it or even   lock the door. I will help my father
into the truck.   The dog will ride in the back where she'll keep an eye
on the fire until it becomes   a star. When we get to town, I'll find us
a room. Maybe two.   I know a lot of songs.

The Legend Of Joe

Once there was a man who worked in a lab
because God is less ugly in a microscope

The man spoke unto a mouse & the mouse
did dance the terrible dance of prophesy
& the man did check his watch & drink
of the dark vessel & put numbers in a book

Once there was a God who worked in a man
as in a sweat-shop making designer clothes,
saying unto them, Your beauty is greater
than your worth

God spoke unto the man & the man did
slouch in the doorway of his long home
& God did check the sun & blow upon
the sea & put his number in all blood

There shall be a lab of machines & they
shall render mice for the stories of men
& the road shall give up its dead & cars
find their own bodies & traffic lights
change to gold & change no more

JOE AGAIN

JOE:
You gotta eat.

THE OLD MAN:
Joe…

JOE:
You gotta play cards.

THE OLD MAN
Joe…

JOE:
The woman's on TV
who looks like mom.

THE OLD MAN:
Joe…

JOE:
OK. Go…

THE OLD MAN:
Where's your brother?

JOE:
He's on another show.

The Formalities

My mother ate Queen Anne

cherries unwashed and smoked
Prince Albert Tobacco.
    A man in a black suit
moved into her chest with a dog
    that had no voice.

At night the man dragged
    furniture or hammered
nails, the dog gasped
    if a siren passed.
Soon after, my mother burned down.
    No one got out.

My brother once held up

     five liquor stores in one
day with a water gun.
     It went pretty well, though
he was forced to shoot the last clerk
  to get away.

When he got home he fell
     asleep with money spread
all over his pillow.
     On the night stand the gun
leaked until it flooded the room
     and he drowned.

My father used to swim

for a living. He dove
on sunken war ships in
    the harbour of Tangiers.
Once he saw a real mermaid
    and she smiled

like my mother. He knew
    his wife must be pregnant
so he came home early.
    When he got there, he found
he'd been divorced for thirty years,
    his sons mermen.

You

are a little ship
that brings its own fog bank.
I am a fireman
smoking in a bookstore.
Together we are Hawaii
rehearsing steam.

In other words, we're good
to go. You row, I'll burn.
You turn, I'll read aloud.
You shroud, I'll steer & shift.
You drift and I'll Continental.
Let's go gentle.

Go gentle,

officer,
my brother is sleeping
& dreaming of breaking
no law. Give him tonight,
tomorrow they're setting his jaw.
Leave him to me,

I promise to tell him
you care. I'll explain, too
why you pulled out his hair.
I'm sure he'll be sorry
but grateful to learn you were fair.
Good luck, out there.

Out there the words are black

        handed boys in T-shirts,
they are skin headed girls
        in tartan skirts, jack boots,
& Dutch up to their squints. It hurts
        to write them out,

to say them to dead dogs,
        to repeat for the cops
so they can get them down
        like pills that do nothing
for grief but give it an echo
        that does not rhyme.

Grief

is a dog that walks
itself to be gassed,
to be passed, or last
thing said to the red clock
by the bed. I say Tornado
and it says No.

I say Earthquake, it shakes
its eyeless head. I say
Fire, it brings a stick
for me to throw, for it
to hunt blind, for it not to find,
to not bring back.

Bring the old man downstairs,

I have to start dinner.
Try to go up noisy,
    make the stairs creak, give him
some small way to know you're coming,
    some thing to solve.

Slide your right arm under
    his knees, your left across
his back, lift when he says,
    and look him in the eye.
Don't tell him he isn't heavy.
    It would kill him.

I don't remember why

I took this job. I think
it had something to do
    with making up for all
the grace I couldn't find for two men
    and a woman.

How many dogs make one
    woman? How many birds
a father and son? How
    do I uncurve the field
in a plow horse's eye and not
    ruin the horse?

Consider the spiders

The spider above you
and all her rationed dead,
    the spider before her
deported in a water glass
    to the front yard.

She didn't make it back.
    Consider her children,
her belongings, her dry
    body reconsidered
by air: flower skeleton,
    umbrella seed.

The Japanese beetle

is deathly allergic
to geranium leaves
    but eats them anyway.
This can put it into coma
    for a whole day.

Given a choice between
    a linden and stupor,
survival and blackout,
    it chooses the latter.
I can't believe Science doesn't
    understand this.

Understand this,

        I don't
   believe in poetry
the way most people do.
   The words never leave me
without taking something with them,
   something heavy.

While I stand here, feeling
   all my pockets for holes
or counting the silver,
   the words are spending me.
My name is Calamity Joe,
   for what it's worth.

─The Charm─

"So I prophesied as I was commanded: and as I prophesied, there was a noise, and behold a rattling, and the bones came together, bone to his bone."
                                    —Ezekiel 37:7

SHIP YOUR HORSE

"Shipping a horse 10 hours, you shouldn't have to oil it,"
—from an equestrian website

ship your horse / put it in a suitcase / shaped

like a horse / THIS END AWAY / ginger ale

is a good way to prep them / maybe a week /

they fuss less / pass easy / hotel water tastes

of hotel sleep / blown / fleeting / go & tell

the horses they're leaving / give them time

to gather themselves / nothing like watching

a horse as the ocean goes by / each wave

a hill / each valley a valley / un-trod /

& the smell / start reading aloud a few days

before you go / something / anything about

shipping / logs / manifests / Treasure Island /

they all love Treasure Island / calms them

right down / except mustangs / give them

how-to's / how to change broken bulbs /

cooking with wild herbs / stars & sextants /

every horse is an ocean turned inside out /

scooping home on its four shells

New Math

Once I asked
myself out
on a date.

Lunch, nothing
big. I had to
say, No.

It wasn't that I
didn't like me.
I do.

Just not that way.

I took it hard.
That night
I dialed

my number ten
times. It was
always busy.

I must have been
screening my
calls.

Who can blame me?

But, it's all right
now, because
I'm friends.

The only time it's
at all awkward
is in public,

when strange men
approach me
and say,

Excuse me, are you sisters?

The Legend Of Joe

Once there was a man who worked in a lab
because his mother died She said marriage
gave her cancer The man wasn't sure
this was true His brother thought it was
hilarious & laughed so hard he drowned
His father said he only meant to take her
dancing
                    The man's heart was a bag
of children's sculpture Whenever he wore
his white coat, a dinosaur broke its neck

One day a nine-fingered girl came to work
in the lab The man could not stop looking
at her, at her hand, the ghost in her glove
If he tried to look away his dinosaurs needed
to dry again on the sill
                           He was deep in love
the way some people are deep in the earth
He asked her dancing & whether she missed
raising her pinky to drink tea
                                  She said no,
she just raised the next finger over & yes,
she loved to dance the way some folks loved
to blame their families for cancer Just then
a team of child archaeologists burst out
of the man's coat & argued down the hall

My Favorite Story Is This One

        where a little blond girl attacks
a family of bears; trashes their home,
eats their food, then runs away
                 feeling invaded
My favorite part comes after the end
when the father bear wordlessly repairs
a little chair, a nail held in his black lip,
the mother wipes a table
            with a checkered rag,
& the cub dries his eyes at a window,
watchful ever after
            for a golden anyone

The Body

The body no longer
matters; the hide,
bones, a gold tooth—
things you'd find
in a racoon's wallet.

I had it wrong.

The heart is not
caged like an animal,
but like a liquor store.
It is caged because
of the men who wait
all night for it to open.

Desire is not a thirst
or even a hotel fire.
It is a coat pocket
searched repeatedly
for a response
to one's name.

The body is to burn
or it is to bury. It is
to be blown apart

or scavenged. The body
is checked for bodies
and roped off.

Bag the body.

The point is the act
of the body; it was here,
it looked like me,
you waved.

A Brief History of The Theater

The first hand puppets were a pair

of hands; no one could agree who

was speaking. Some saw a swan,

some a crocodile. None saw the king.

Many just stared at the puppeteer,

terrified, unready for show business.

A few, treacherous few, understood

too well: make shadows of the truth

& it can't be traced back. It needed

a lot of work. The critics hung him

on the city wall. Later a child noticed

if you climbed up & shook the rope,

it looked like the man was dancing.

Tragoedia

Because the ant may lift twenty times itself,
it must. The honeybee dies only of work
or murder. The queen is mother to most
of her army, but a spider has no relations
in any book, no link to another spinning
thing. Whatever orbits earth, even on legs,
is a moon; the first tragedy. It's too much
for the lemming. Too much for the eagle,
who must mate while falling, sometimes
falling all the way. The platypus sleeps
seventeen hours a day, daring death to dream
a life less lonely. What is anything to do?
The world keeps happening & the fish
with no memory, the crocodile no tongue,
the giraffe no voice, the goat no song, the lion
& wolf no color in their eyes, the rabbit
no tears, no tears.

Flight Out of Guest Bedroom

The only book in this house—
Controlling The Japanese Beetle,
the only door she leaves unlocked.
I can feel her guarding her garden,

controlling the Japanese beetle,
the earthworm, the fervid peach,
while she sleeps upstairs, sown
in the mattress like Kansas.

The earthworm, blind as the peach,
stays up reading about poison,
in bed with its Braille map of America,
unfolded and unfolded and unfolded;

I stay up, poisoned with reading
how to confuse the Japanese beetle
by turning and returning the land
with milk. My aunt hoards sleep,

dreams her irregular heartbeat will
throw off poachers. I go down the hall
for milk, creep the boards awhile.
She's left nothing for me to open.

It's how she loves me, off and down,
the only door she leaves unlocked.
I'm un-shelved, fallen open,
the last book in this house.

RETREATISE

In these last worlds before the moment ends
I want to confess the gifts of my misuse—
the hole in the wind where the door got in—
nights I lived to promise better, days
I swore all I forgot.

       The only book in my poem,
that means anything, is one where a balloon
loses a child and searches dying for it. Hey!
Ho! The creep is dawning! Any pageant
in the brilliant face of morning can eye
my capture. Mean what I know?

       I want to thank harvest
for every god, each seed and suckling
into a mouthful grown. I never fortuned
where my questions came. Bed for time.
The tired have got stars at last.

The Legend Of Joe

I work in a lab. Sometimes I'm a table,
other times I interview mice. Today
I did eight hours at a microscope,
talking to a virus. Tomorrow I'll judge
what it retains. I live in a burning house

with my burning father & our burning
ghosts. I play with a burning dog, write
poems to a burning sweetheart, & watch
the town from my window;

                              the blazing cars
& houses, children aflame in the park,
black roads, the life of smoke.

A girl went missing awhile back,
her name is Lily. Everyone dropped
what they were doing to search. Some
say she burned away. Another,
my landlord, says he can see her

in X-rays of his lungs. He'll show
anyone who asks, how to recognize
her silhouette. It looks like a blob
to me, but he says that's because
she's on horseback.

           I'm afraid
of horses, but I went to the florist
and bought a lily to pray over. They
haven't found her; not as many folks
looking.
           I asked the virus if it knew
anything. It didn't say, but was clearly
holding back. There's a boy I might
ask. He's been bugging me for a pet
mouse.
           This isn't going stop,
you know. I haven't even gotten
to my father, yet, how he smolders
in his bed. Or the ghosts, or my love,

or death; how it isn't coming, how it
doesn't come ever. It's here from
the beginning, waiting for us to speak.
It nods to everything we say.

JOE ONE MORE TIME

JOE:
This is our house.

THE NINE-FINGERED GIRL:
Nice house.

JOE:
These are our dead.

THE NINE-FINGERED GIRL:
Nice to meet you.

JOE:
This is your seat.

THE NINE-FINGERED GIRL:
Don't mind if I do.

JOE:
There was a dog. I mean, a boy.
He was like a flower. He drowned.
Then another, like a deer. He ran away.

THE NINE-FINGERED GIRL:
Which way?

JOE:
The way you came.

THE NINE-FINGERED GIRL:
After you.

The Calm

A dead man doesn't walk into a bar

The bartender doesn't hear his order,

even with the television turned down.

A dead man doesn't ask for change

to make a call. The phone rings.

The bartender answers, says, *Nope,*

haven't seem him yet, turns back

to the TV. A barn is burning there;

horses kick out their stalls. A woman

searches the blaze, calls out a word,

does it again, the same word because

her mouth makes the same shape,

the brief shape of a man's name.

The shape of my name

looks like *Carnation blue*. It is *Good*

to see you, and even *Damned if I do*.

But it also resembles *Come on and go*,

Animal show, and *Whatayaknow*.

I say it to the rusty veins of my mother's

hand-mirror, a little slower each time,

until my mouth looks like her mouth.

I say police and it looks like *please*,

my old man looks like *my old man*, but

brother could be *nothing*. With practice

I'll say it so easily you'll swear

I'm only breathing.

Swear

you will sleep half your sleep.

Swear, double swear it. The monkeys

will spare us, the rabbits forgive us,

& white-stallion-mice bear the virus

away. Triple swear on your daddy's

toupee, on his one good eye, his mouth—

full of momma; you saw her ghost

& she was happy as hell to be seen.

Swear that your other hand's clean.

On a stack of crackers, a river of wine,

sweet baby Jesus with salt & lime,

swear your tongue is fatter than mine.

The boy in the next room is mine

Possession is nine tenths of dolor;

his bike is tied to the hood of my car.

I found him working Sixth Street, adrift

between the red and white lights,

pretending to be tired of farms, instead

of pretending. He's waiting for me

to come out with a beer, with how I want

him. I don't. He was the closest thing

to a deer I could find in town, makes

the room wild. I'll watch him drink

& let him go. Then stare at his cup,

at the air he took up. *God damn . . .*

Which brings us to God

On the first day He made light, but took it

away that night. Too early to see a pattern,

no one to see it. Today He made the police

return my brother's clothes: one T-shirt,

one pair of pants, no shorts, no shoes, odd

socks. Did God tell him what to wear?

Did He speak unto my brother, saying

"Dress light, dress for summer. And take

Joe's college ring, it balances the slacks.

He won't be mad, the cops'll give it back."

I'm going to make my dad a drink, tell him

the truth, there was no one at the door.

How many doors

can't be answered

in a lifetime? When our cat died, dad said

it went to live with relatives in Egypt.

Mother liked an open door, hid nothing:

Your brother's a drunk, Your father's

penis looks like a closed lily, My body

was flawless until you pulled it apart.

Lab mice can't see doors. I spare them

only the big stuff: *You'll love the dunes,*

the pyramids are beautiful at dawn

& dusk. A good lie is made of wood.

Truth only muscle. No bone.

I've found an answer in the bones,

in the Hebrew bones of mice. I asked

them to confess their cancer. The answer

was *No*. I'm revising the question

for a millionth time, just in case the bones

are slow. A new injectionist, a girl,

has named the alpha mouse Ezekiel,

in hopes his bones will show the sins

of their Israel. The pinky of her left hand

is gone. She says she lost it cutting flowers

as a child, says it still sends messages home,

something about sand. I watch that hand

in its glove all day, one finger full of breath.

I dreamt I was your finger,

the one you lost as a kid, clipping roses

with your mother. It began with falling

from your hand, from the dripping V

of the shears. I landed in the ripe mud

forgetting, who I was leaking out in pulses:

I am a girl. I was a girl. Whose thoughts

are these? The dark, the dark. The earth

carried your voices, I could feel myself

talked about, looked for, not found,

though I pointed & pointed. I'm coming

back to you, slowly like an arrow shot

underground. I woke knowing this.

Know this:

a poem isn't a story, two make

a valley, three a constellation, four or more

a gallery at best. At worst a gang of boys

casing the neighborhood for a dark house.

It isn't safe, it never was. My old man

sleeps later and later, his face pointed down

to the left, the artery in his neck thumping

like a lost guest behind a curtain. Policemen

read body language as a line. They'd say,

whatever he's dreaming, it's a lie. I wish

it were. A story is a house told by rooms;

a poem one window flooded with light.

Poem

How old are the chairs in chair-years?

Are they younger or older than we?

If a nine-fingered girl came to diner,

on what side should her silverware be?

The old man's in his bathrobe & necktie;

he's come all the way from his bed.

The rest of the family can't make it

they're busy tonight being dead.

If the nine-fingered girl gets here early

will I hear her climbing the stair?

I'd run but I have me surrounded.

Come out with my hands in the air!

The boy has come back,

the boy

from the night-market of Sixth Street

is at the door with his bicycle & his eye

black as quarry mud. He won't face me,

speaks to my neck, shoulders down,

ready to close. I want to say this right:

he looks like someone stole his antlers,

like lamplight is heavy, like a photograph

of a photograph. He says some men tried

to eat him. He remembers that I fed him.

Can he sleep here? Maybe live here?

Do I have anything to cover his eye?

Cover your eyes,

while I change

into my old man, my crack boy,

my chipped girl. I'll put on my horse

& monkey, my comfy room, get

tight in the family Africa, slip on

some shepherds, don my cradle.

Don't look until I say, until I say

giddy up, until your hands get hot

on your face & the landlord asks

how you got in, what you're doing

in this house alone.

Dies Irae *(Day of Wrath)*

Tear open the zinnia
Break open the hive
Loot each comb of its heavy flame,
Give it all to the mud

Let lightning come,
Let trees be wounded,
Birds pour from their hairy goblets,
Sing singly

OK, OK, Whateveryousay

Start a bath for the moon
A coffin for the sun
Gather clouds to witness
The reading of the wind's will

Unname the comets
Unnumber the stars
Don't help if night stumbles
Look away when it falls

May the lion lie down
With the waitress,
The brown bear sleep
With the watchman

May the planets blow
Back to their glittery husks,
The sky at last be closed
as a bog potato's eye

Let no new word be found
or written in the book
of the laboratory mouse

Biographical Note

Brendan Constantine's work has appeared in numerous journals, most notably *Ploughshares, FIELD, The Pinch, RATTLE, Ninth Letter, The Los Angeles Review, PANK, Redivider, RUNES,*and the LA *Times* best-seller *The Underground Guide To Los Angeles.* He is the author of two previous collections: *Letters To Guns* (2009 Red Hen Press) and *Birthday Girl With Possum* (2011 Write Bloody Publishing).

Mr. Constantine is poet-in-residence at the Windward School in West Los Angeles. In addition, he regularly conducts workshops for foster care centers, hospitals, and with the Alzheimer's Poetry Project.